Skin Deep

Annette Capone
Orig. title: Best Face Forward

SCHOLASTIC INC.
New York Toronto London Auckland Sydney

ISBN 0-590-33458-1

12 11 10 9 8 7   4 5/9

• TABLE OF CONTENTS •

Wildfire Extras

You and Your Hair
  by Elaine Budd
Your 14-Day Total Shape-up
  by Annette Capone
How To Be a Teen Model
  by Jane Claypool Miner
The Wildfire Romance Fill-in Book
  by Julie Frankel and Michael Scheier
Skin Deep
  by Annette Capone

· ONE ·

Getting to Know Your Skin

Is a prettier, healthier-looking complexion something you would like to have? You *can* change the skin you're in. Even if your skin's flaws seem major to you, it's possible to fight back and win. So whatever your skin problem is don't let it get you down. *Take charge.*

Are you constantly battling with blemishes? Then the oil on your face is the enemy, because there's too much of it. Find out how to give your skin a healthy shine without causing greasiness. Is your skin supersensitive? You can control blotches and redness with special routines. If your skin is extra-dry in spots but shiny and slick in others, you'll find just the right treatment in this book.

Your skin is the result of heredity and the victim of environment. You can't change what nature gave you, but you *can* learn how to cope with your skin and make a significant difference in its appearance once you do.

You can also learn to cope with your environment so that it takes less of a toll on your skin. Face-saving techniques can help your skin survive hot summer sun, cold and dry winter air, heat and humidity, and even pollution.

For starters, evaluate your skin care routine. If your complexion is all you'd like it to be, then the treatment you're giving it is probably just fine. But if there's something about your skin that you'd like to change, then a change in routine is in order. With just a little more effort and discipline, you can design a brand-new skin care routine that's perfect for you in every way.

This book will teach you the right way to cleanse and moisturize your complexion. You'll learn how to deal with its special problems, and to pamper it when necessary.

You'll also discover that you can change your skin from the inside out by eating foods that actually nourish your skin. When you take charge and balance your diet, you'll soon be eating what your skin needs.

You will learn how to change your skin with makeup, too. With just a few tips and tricks, you can put on makeup that improves your looks and brings out your best features. Step by step, you'll discover how to choose and use makeup products like a pro.

You will find out that exercise makes a big difference in your complexion. When your body's in shape, your skin shows it. Exercise will rev up your circulation, relax your muscles, and get your skin glowing. One good workout a day will give your skin the blush of good health — the best blush of all.

Know your skin

Before you begin your new skin regimen, you have to get to know your skin type. Think of yourself as a scientist: Your mission is to identify your skin's personality; test treatments that have worked on complexions similar to yours; and experiment until you come up with the skin care regimen that leaves your skin prettier and healthier looking.

Below are four checklists to help you figure out what kind of skin you have. Check off any statements that apply to your skin.

BOX A:

___Enlarged pores plague you.

___Blackheads are a constant nuisance.

___A super-shiny face is something you've learned to live with.

___Pimples pop up too frequently.

___Tiny bumps make their home under your skin.

___Blotchy, uneven color is a problem.

_____Your makeup runs — fast — and turns colors.

_____Your hair is so slick you have to shampoo every day.

_____Your face is sticky to the touch and perspires a lot.

_____Flakiness is a recurring problem.

BOX B:

_____Shine is rare — dull is a better description.

_____Your skin is rough to the touch — rarely smooth.

_____Your skin feels tight and taut.

_____Your skin chaps easily in cold weather.

_____Flakiness is a year-round woe.

_____Your skin super-sensitive and you don't know why.

_____You get sunburned easily.

_____Pimples crop up, but not too often.

_____Color is ashy, uneven, or sometimes red in spots.

BOX C:

_____Blemishes are a rare occurrence.

_____Your skin looks and feels smooth more often than not.

_____Pores are practically invisible.

_____Color is even all over your face.

_____Occasionally your skin feels sensitive, but not often.

_____Soap and water works wonders for you.

4

___In the cold, your face glows and doesn't chap or flake.
___Blackheads are unknown to you.
___The shine on your face is just right.
_•_Makeup stays on until you take it off.

BOX D:

___Nose, forehead, chin, and mouth area are pimple-prone.
___Your face shines in the same places.
___Enlarged pores and blackheads describe the skin on your nose.
___Cheeks flake or chap frequently.
___After washing with soap and water, you need a heavy moisturizer.
___You shampoo frequently and your bangs get especially greasy.
___Often your makeup turns color.

How did you score?

Count the number of checks you made in each box. Which one has the highest number? That box, below, describes your skin type.

BOX A: OILY SKIN

Oily skin doesn't last forever, but at this time in your life it can be a problem. Your sebaceous, or oil glands, are overactive right now. Most likely, you inherited this tendency. As a result, your pores are clogged and enlarged. When that excess oil darkens and dries, blackheads crop up. When it combines with bacteria and dead skin cells, it comes out as pimples. And when the oil just lies there, sticking to dead skin cells, your oily skin can look as flaky as dry skin, yet feel sticky as well.

The wrong cleansing routine, a poor diet, tension, heat, sun, and humidity can all make oil glands even more active. Your aim is to get rid of all that extra oil without stripping your skin of the moisture it needs.

BOX B: DRY SKIN

Your complexion lacks the moisture it needs to look its best. That's because your sebaceous, or oil glands are sluggish, a condition you probably inherited. The oil on your face seals in your skin's natural moisture. Without that light coating of oil, the moisture you need evaporates. Sun, dry, cold air, poor diet, tension, and the incorrect cleansing routines may aggravate your problem. Your goal is to give your skin what nature didn't: moisture, but you have to know exactly how to do that. Overdo it and you'll clog your pores with grease, ending up with seemingly oily skin problems, such as blackheads, even pimples.

BOX C: NORMAL SKIN

Your skin has exactly what it needs to look and feel healthy. It's neither too dry nor too oily, but somewhere in between. Most likely you inherited your fine complexion, so consider yourself lucky. Of course, you want to give your skin the best possible care so that it will always be as nice as it is right now. And, if you are occasionally bothered by blackheads and pimples, as most teens are, you want to know how to get rid of them fast. Your goal is to maintain your well-balanced skin and learn how to handle any minor problems that crop up.

BOX D: COMBINATION SKIN

Oily in spots, dry or normal in others, your skin is a combination of types — and the trickiest type to handle. In most combination complexions, there's excess oil in the T-zone formed by your forehead, nose, and chin. That's where the sebaceous, or oil, glands are most often overactive, producing so much oil that it clogs your pores. If the oil sticks around too long, it will dry up and change color, forming blackheads. Or it might mix with bacteria and dead skin cells, overstuffing your pores and causing a whitehead or pimple.

You may have inherited your combination skin, or it may be just a temporary condition during your teen years, when all your glands are working overtime. A poor diet, tension, the wrong cleansing routine, heat, sun, humidity, and cold dry air can all aggravate your problem.

The rest of your face may be normal or on the dry side. That means you have to treat each part differently. Your goal is to remove the excess oil from your T-zone and add moisture to those parts of your face that look and feel thirsty — tricky, but it can be done.

The paper test

Still unsure what type of skin you have? Then take the paper test:

Wash your face with your usual soap and warm water. Rinse about twenty times using warm water. Don't put anything at all on your skin. After one or two hours take five small pieces of ordinary brown paper (the kind used for bags and packages) and wipe one across your forehead, another across your nose, one across your chin, and one across each side of your face. Oil will darken the brown paper, even make it translucent.

Which parts of your face are oiliest? Driest? If all the papers are greasy, you have oily skin. Some greasy and some not means you have combination skin. No grease at all? Your complexion is dry. Just a bit of oil all over? Your skin is quite normal.

What's under the skin?

If you're going to seek the perfect treatment for your skin by experimenting with many treatments, then you must get your facts straight. Here's what you need to know:

The skin you see is merely the outer layer, called the epidermis. It consists of many thin layers of cells that were formed deep under the epidermis. These cells have worked themselves up to the surface. The epidermis can have only four or five layers (as on your eyelid) or as many as one hundred layers (as does the skin on the soles of your feet). The epidermis on your face is usually about fifteen to thirty layers deep. By the time the skin cells that make up the epidermis are on the visible surface, they are actually dead and ready to flake off. As dead cells flake off, or are rubbed or washed away, new cells rise to take their place, so that your skin is constantly renewing itself. In fact, you get a new outer skin every twenty-seven days or so.

Pores are the visible, topmost part of tiny canals, called follicles, that run through the epidermis from the inner layers of the skin. These follicles are the openings of sweat and oil glands. They deposit your natural oils and perspiration on the skin surface all day long.

The purpose of washing your face is to remove dead skin cells, bacteria, excess oil, and perspiration, as well as any surface dirt and makeup. You don't want to overwash and strip your skin of all its natural oils, which are needed to lock in moisture. And you don't want to underwash and leave a residue of grease, bacteria, and perspiration, which can only clog up your pores and lead to skin woes. The next chapter tells you the best techniques for cleaning your unique skin type.

· TWO ·

Super-Clean is Super-Beautiful

Clear, smooth, terrific-looking skin starts with a top-notch cleansing routine. Just washing your face regularly isn't nearly enough. Your routine doesn't have to be complicated, but you must use the proper products, tools, and techniques.

It's easy to become an expert. All the basic information you need starts here. You'll find out how to cleanse your skin, using a method designed for your skin type. With a few minor changes, you will be able to create a routine that's tailor-made for you. You can do that by experimenting until you discover exactly what products, tools, and techniques give you the best results.

The top cleansers

To get your skin really clean you must have the right cleansers. Here are the different kinds available to you.

Soaps

They're not all alike. Some soaps will be better for your type skin than others.

Oily skin. Avoid cream and oil-based soaps. If your skin is excessively greasy, use one that was created for oily skin. Just read the labels. Occasionally you may want to use an abrasive soap, which contains tiny granules that slough off dead skin cells, loosen oil from clogged pores, and stimulate circulation for a healthy glow.

Dry skin. If your skin is especially dry and sensitive, you may find that you cannot use soap at all. In that case, you should try a cleansing lotion (more on that coming up). But usually you can use an oil- or cream-based soap. Read the labels and choose a soap that was created for your skin type. Glycerin-based soaps are gentle on your skin and will most likely not cause any irritation or chapping.

Normal skin. Use any mild soap. Sample a few until you find the right one for you. You may also use a cleansing lotion if you prefer that to soap. If your skin feels tight and dry after you wash with soap, then switch to a brand designed for drier skin. If you feel your soap isn't getting your skin clean enough, then it's probably too greasy for you.

Sensitive skin. Dry, oily, or normal, some skin types are particularly sensitive to soap. The solution is to try one that's hypoallergenic, which means that the soap contains no perfumes or irritants, such as detergents. You might like one that's glycerin-based.

TIP: If your area has very hard water, the minerals in it can combine with your soap to leave a residue on your skin. Rinsing with water may not be enough. You might also have to use an astringent, toner, or freshener after you wash (more on those later).

Cleansing lotions

These are to be used instead of soap. It's just a matter of preference, because soap and lotions basically do the same job. Some cleansing lotions are supposed to be used with water; others are to be applied with cotton balls and wiped off with tissues or more cotton balls. Some lather; others don't. There are cleansing lotions made for every type of skin. Some are designed to be used together with a toner (for normal to dry skin) or an astringent (for oily skin).

Cleansing creams

These are made from fats, oils, and water — for example, plain old cold cream. No matter what type of skin you have, you ought to use a cleansing cream to remove your makeup, particularly your eye makeup.

You should never try to rub off eye makeup with soap and a wash-cloth. It's much too harsh a technique to use on such a sensitive part of your face. Also, soap cannot always take off greasy dirt, unless it's very strong (which sometimes means too harsh for your skin type). Just pat a little cleansing cream around your eyes, then gently rub off makeup with a tissue or cotton ball. Be careful not to smudge cream all over your face (especially if your skin is oily, because you don't need more grease).

The film that remains after you remove your makeup with cleansing cream must be washed away.

Astringents, toners, and fresheners

Telling them apart can be confusing, and sometimes the labels are no help at all. Just remember this: the difference is only in the amount of alcohol each contains.

Astringents contain the most alcohol, which is a potent grease-cutter, so it ought to be used by those with *oily skin*. If you have *combination skin*, use an astringent only on the oily areas. An astringent tightens your pores as it removes excess oil and so helps prevent blackheads and pimples. In addition to the commercial brands, witch hazel and ordinary rubbing alcohol are excellent astringents. Use an astringent if you wash your face with a cleansing lotion. You don't have to use one if you wash with soap, but you may find it's a good idea, especially if you have acne. Any astringent should be used after you have removed your makeup and washed your face. Apply with cotton balls and stay away from the area around your eyes. Do not rinse with water.

Toners are terrific for *normal skin*. They cut grease and take away any traces of makeup and soap, which are drying, leaving your skin looking and feeling refreshed. Use a toner if your skin feels tight after you wash with soap or a cleansing lotion. Just apply with cotton balls. Do not rinse with water.

Fresheners contain the least amount of alcohol. Because they are so gentle, they are best for *dry, sensitive skin*. They, too, are refreshing and help remove any traces of makeup, soap, and grime. Fresheners are optional, but do use one if your skin feels too dry after you wash with soap, or whenever you use a cleansing lotion. Fresheners should not be rinsed off with water.

Wash that face!

Oily skin wash-up

You want to get your skin clean, of course, but not squeaky clean. If you remove too much oil by overwashing and overscrubbing, you will only create more problems for yourself. Your skin needs some natural oils to seal in the moisture, which keeps it looking dewy and healthy.

To control oil, washing three times a day is probably sufficient: once in the morning, again in the afternoon—removing makeup completely and reapplying, and finally at night, so that you go to sleep with clean skin.

Here are tips to help you do the job correctly. Remember, you will have to experiment until you discover the routine that's perfect for you. How to tell? By the positive results you're getting.

1. Remove any eye makeup. Just put a spot of light cleansing cream on your brow bone and, using a tissue or cotton ball, gently wipe off your eye makeup.

Be thorough, yet be careful not to spread the cream to other parts of your face. You don't need any extra grease! Even if your skin is extremely oily, don't remove eye makeup with soap and a washcloth. Soap is too drying and irritating for the thin, sensitive skin around your eyes, and a washcloth, no matter how clean, may harbor bacteria or spread it around. Also, rubbing with a washcloth can be irritating to the eye area. So do use a cream. You can find one that's not too greasy; some are even made for oily skin.

2. *Always use warm water.* Hot water will only activate your oil glands, and cold water won't cut the grease.

3. *Don't forget your neck* and even your shoulders when working up a lather.

4. *Use your fingers*, never a washcloth, to apply the soap. Massage lightly. Do not allow lather to touch the eye area, which is sensitive and, even on the oiliest skin, needs all the moisture it can get.

5. *Lather up and rinse.* And then lather up and rinse again. Always rinse in clear running water about twenty times — ten times with warm water and ten times with slightly cool water (never cold). Pat your skin dry with a clean towel (never rub).

6. *Change your soap occasionally.* Your skin might get used to one brand, and it will no longer be as effective. Always use a soap or cleansing lotion created for oily skin. Once a week you might try a medicated soap, which often contains acne-fighting ingredients, or an abrasive soap, which will slough off dead skin cells that may have accumulated on the surface of your skin. Also, as a

rule, it takes about two weeks to know if a soap is right for you. If, after two weeks, you find the soap irritating or the results disappointing, switch to another brand.

7. *Apply your astringent.* Or you could add a teaspoon of lemon juice, a good natural degreaser, to a basin of cool water and rinse your skin about five to ten times.

8. *Use light moisturizer around your eyes.* Unless your skin is excessively oily, you may put a light moisturizer on your skin, especially if you wear face makeup. Try wearing a moisturizer for two weeks, then go two weeks without, and see what your skin likes best.

9. *Apply a mask for oily skin* once a week. Every other week, or as often as you find necessary and helpful, give yourself a steam facial. More on masks and facials coming up.

10. *Between face washings* during the day, dab your skin with astringent towelettes or blotting papers to wipe away excess oil. Don't use powder, which will make your skin sticky and clog your pores.

11. *Shampoo your hair every day.* Most likely, if your skin is oily, your hair is oily, too, and the oil on the hair surrounding your face will find its way to your facial skin. If you simply can't shampoo, at least wash your bangs with soap and water, shampoo, or a dry shampoo.

Dry skin wash-up

You want to wash away dirt and grime and bacteria without stripping your skin of its natural oils. Do it with a gentle touch and gentle products. Then, occasionally, give your skin special treatment to get rid of any dry and flaky patches.

Usually, dry skin need be washed only twice a day. In the morning, splashing on warm water may be all that's necessary. But do wash your face midday, taking off and reapplying makeup, and in the evening before you go to sleep.

Here's how to do the job correctly. Keep in mind that you must experiment until you find the cleansing routine that leaves your skin clean but not drier than it already is.

1. Remove your eye makeup. Just put a spot of cleansing cream on your brow bone and, using a tissue or cotton ball, very gently wipe off your makeup. You could also use petroleum jelly.

Never remove your eye makeup with soap and a washcloth. Soap is too drying for the delicate skin around your eyes and a washcloth may harbor bacteria. Also, a rubbing with a washcloth can be irritating, especially for dry, sensitive skin.

2. Always wash with warm water. Temperature extremes will only irritate your dry, sensitive skin and may leave it even dryer.

3. Use your fingers to apply the soap, massaging your skin with light strokes. Do not allow the lather to touch your eye area, which is probably the driest area on your face. Most cleansing lotions should be applied with your fingers, too.

Once a week, and not more often, you may use a very clean washcloth as part of your routine. To remove dead cells, gently rub your skin wherever it is especially flaky. You may use an abrasive soap made for dry skin types.

4. Lather up and rinse. And then lather up and rinse again. Always rinse in clear running water about twenty times — ten times with warm water and ten times with slightly cool, but not cold, water. Pat your skin dry (never rub) with a clean towel.

5. Apply your freshener. Or, if your face feels taut, add a teaspoon of apple cider vinegar to a basin of warm water and rinse about five to ten times. Try a freshener, or vinegar rinse for about two weeks. If your face feels better without it, then you can skip this step.

6. Use light moisturizer all over your face. During the winter when the air is drying, and at night if you feel you need it, use a heavier moisturizer, then blot with a tissue. But never use a heavy moisturizer under face makeup. It will only clog your pores and cause blackheads and pimples.

7. Give yourself a moisturizing mask once a week. And every two weeks, a steam facial for dry skin. More on masks and facials coming up.

8. A few final tips: Carry your moisturizer with you during the day so you can dab a little on when your face looks and feels dry. During the winter, keep a shallow pan of water near your room's heating unit in order to keep the air moist. Or invest in an inexpensive humidifier. Never use face powder because it is drying. Do use a shampoo made for dry hair — dry skin and hair often go together.

Combination skin wash-up

Your goal is to clean your face all over and, at the same time, remove the excess oil from your T-zone only. You don't want to strip the other areas of the oil needed to seal in moisture. The trick is to wash different parts of your face differently. It's a cinch, once you have the know-how.

To keep the oil in check, you ought to wash your face three times a day: once in the morning, again in the afternoon, removing your makeup and reapplying it, and finally in the evening, before you go to bed.

Because every combination of types is somewhat unique, you must experiment and try various routines until you discover the one that suits your skin best. Two weeks on a routine should tell. If, at the end of that time, you aren't getting positive results, make one small change in the routine. Two weeks later, if you are still dissatisfied, make another change. You may find the ideal face-washing technique sooner than you think. Here are some guidelines.

1. Remove your eye makeup. Put a spot of cleansing cream on your brow bone and, with a tissue or cotton ball, carefully wipe off your eye makeup. You could also use petroleum jelly.

Be very careful not to spread the cream to other parts of your face, particularly the T-zone, which doesn't need any extra oil. Never use soap and a washcloth to remove makeup because it's too harsh and drying for the sensitive area around your eyes. You can find creams that are not too greasy; some are even made for oily skin.

2. Always use warm water. Hot water stimulates the oil glands and cold water can't cut the grease on your face.

3. Use a soap or cleansing lotion created for normal skin. One that's designed for oily skin might be too harsh for the dry or normal parts of your face, and one that's designed for dry skin won't be strong enough to remove the grease from your T-zone. Try a soap for about two weeks. If you find the results disappointing — if it leaves your skin feeling oily or too taut — then switch to another brand.

Once a week, use a medicated soap, which contains acne-fighting ingredients, or an abrasive soap, which contains tiny granules that slough off dead skin cells.

4. Apply soap with your fingers, never a washcloth. Massage your skin lightly, especially around the T-zone. Do not allow the lather to touch the eye area, which is sensitive and needs all the oil it can get.

5. Lather up and rinse. And then lather up and rinse again. Always rinse in clear running water about twenty times — ten times with warm water and ten times with slightly cool water, never too cold. Pat your skin dry with a fresh towel (never rub).

6. Apply your astringent to the oily parts of your face, using a cotton ball. Do not rinse off.

7. Apply a light moisturizer only where needed: under your eyes, around the mouth, on your cheeks, for example. During the day, if you wear face makeup, you might try a light moisturizer all over your face. Test the moisturizer for two weeks, then go two weeks without moisturizer, and see what your skin likes best.

8. Apply a mask for oily skin on your T-zone once a week. Every other week, or as often as you find necessary and helpful, give yourself a steam facial. More on masks and facials coming up.

9. *Between face washings* during the day, dab your oily skin with astringent towelettes or blotting papers. Don't use powder, which will only make your skin sticky and clog your pores, causing blackheads and pimples.

10. *Shampoo your hair every day* if it's oily because the oil on the hair surrounding your face will find its way to your forehead and cheeks. If you can't shampoo, at least wash your bangs with soap and water, your regular shampoo, or a dry shampoo.

Normal skin wash-up

Your skin is well-balanced, neither too oily nor too dry, and you want to keep it that way. If your cleansing routine isn't just right, you can tip the scales and lose that balance. A soap that's too harsh, for example, can cause your skin to flake. If you overwash and overscrub you can irritate your skin. If you don't wash your skin often enough or thoroughly enough, you can get some of the problems usually found in oily skin.

Usually normal skin need be washed only twice a day, in the morning and in the evening before you go to bed. When minor problems crop up, such as a few blemishes somewhere in your T-zone, you may also wash midafternoon, removing all your makeup then reapplying it.

As with all other skin types, you must experiment until you find the routine that's perfectly tailored to you. Here are a few pointers.

1. *Remove your eye makeup*, using a cleansing cream or petroleum jelly. Simply put a dab on your brow bone and wipe off with a tissue or cotton ball.

Be gentle. Never use a washcloth to remove eye makeup. And soap is too drying for the delicate skin around your eyes.

2. *Always wash with warm water.* Temperature extremes will irritate your skin. Hot water activates your oil glands.

3. *Use your fingers* to apply the soap, massaging your skin with light strokes. Do not allow the lather to touch your sensitive eye area, which is probably the driest area on your face. Use a mild soap, or one designed for normal skin (read the labels) or a cleansing lotion for normal skin.

4. *Lather up and rinse.* And then lather up and rinse again. Always rinse in clear running water about twenty times — ten times with warm water and ten times with slightly cool, but not cold, water. Pat your skin dry (never rub) with a clean towel.

5. Use a freshener after you wash. Soap can leave a drying film. Try it for about two weeks. If your skin feels too taut, skip this step.

6. Smooth on a light moisturizer all over your face. During the winter when the air is dry, or at night if you feel you need it, use a heavier moisturizer around your eyes and wherever your skin feels tight, then blot with a tissue. Never use a heavy moisturizer under your makeup. It will clog your pores and cause blackheads, even pimples, on the most normal of skins.

7. Give yourself a moisturizing face mask once a week, one that's made for normal skin. Every two weeks — and not more often — try a steam facial. That will help keep your pores as clean and as invisible as they are right now. More on masks and facials coming up.

8. Never use powder. If your skin looks oily in the T-zone, blot with astringent towelettes. If your hair is oily, wash it every day or the oil will spread to your face.

· THREE ·

Special Pampering Treatments

To deep-clean your face and give it the extra ounce of care that can make a big difference in the way it looks and feels, nothing beats a steamy facial. The heat plus the steam will open your pores, loosening any grime, grease, and flakes that have built up. Then all you have to do is gently scrub your skin clean and finally tighten your pores once again. Not only can you learn to give yourself a facial like a pro, you can make everything you need from natural ingredients — stuff that's probably on the shelves in your kitchen and fridge right now. So here's how to pamper your skin quickly, easily and effectively.

The 10-minute step-by-step facial

1. Pull your hair back, away from your face, with a headband or shower cap.

2. Wash your face using your regular soap and warm water. Rinse thoroughly.

3. Fill a medium-size pot with water and heat until it's simmering gently. Never allow the water to boil. Pour that warm water into the bathroom sink.

4. Lean over the sink and drape a large towel over your head so that it forms a tent to prevent the steam from escaping. Be sure your face is at least six inches from the water, and keep your eyes closed.

5. Steam your face for about five minutes. If the water begins to cool add some more hot water straight from the tap.

6. A light scrubbing comes next, to lift off the dirt, oil, and flaky skin the steam heat has loosened. Drain the sink, then wash your face (using your fingertips) with an abrasive soap and warm water. Or you can use a medicated soap. If your skin is extremely flaky, you may use a washcloth, but be sure to use a light touch.

7. Rinse your skin well, at least twenty times, in running water: first warm, then cool — never icy cold.

8. The final step: apply your toner, freshener, or astringent, depending on your skin type. If your skin is dry or normal,

smooth on your moisturizer. For oily skin, a bit of moisturizer around your eye area is all you need.

The 25-minute step-by-step facial

This steam treatment may take a little longer, but if you can find the time, the results are really worth it. Not only is it good for your skin, it's so relaxing, refreshing, reviving, that's it's good for your body and mind, too.

1. Pull your hair back, wash your face as usual, rinse thoroughly, then steam for a full five minutes.
2. Rinse twenty times, with warm, then cool, running water. Don't dry your skin. If your face feels taut, slather on a light moisturizer.
3. Apply a mask, one that was made for your skin type. (There are plenty to choose from; just read the labels. The mask you buy should not only be right for your skin, it must also appeal to your senses. Does it look, smell, and feel good on your face? Keep trying different masks until you find the one that is most effective and most appealing to you.) Do not apply the mask to the area around your eyes and lips. If you have combination skin, use the mask only on the oily parts.

4. Leave the mask on for fifteen minutes, never more than 30 minutes. While you're waiting, lie down with your feet slightly higher than your head. You might also find it soothing to put a cool damp washcloth, or cool damp teabags, over your eyes. Soft and pretty background music may help to make this an even more relaxing experience.
5. When the time is up, rinse your face for a bracing finish: ten times with warm water and ten times with cool.
6. Finally, apply your toner, freshener, or astringent. If your skin is dry to normal, smooth on your moisturizer. If your skin is oily, moisturize only around your eyes. You ought to use a particular kind of mask at least four times before you decide whether it's right for you.

Make your own masks

Raid your kitchen and try a mask every time you give yourself a 25-minute facial. These are fun to put together and they work. Some have astringent qualities to tighten your pores and absorb excess oil. Some clean and moisturize at the same time. Others are slightly granular, good for getting rid of the flakes. All are stimulating so that they rev up your skin and leave you with a rosy glow. Here are the recipes. Each mask should be left on your skin for about fifteen minutes, followed by a rinse as directed.

Masks for oily and combination skin

Egg White. Separate the white from the yolk, putting each in a different small bowl. Beat both slightly. Apply the egg white to your skin. Once it dries slightly, put on another layer. You will find that egg white is a potent astringent.

What to do with the yolk? Put it into two capfuls of your favorite shampoo. It's an excellent body builder for hair.

Oatmeal. Mix ¼ cup oatmeal with enough warm water to form a thick paste.

Variations: Substitute wheat germ, bran, cornmeal, or almond meal for the oatmeal. One of these is sure to become your favorite.

If your skin is extra oily, add 1 teaspoon of lemon juice, witch hazel, or baking soda.

Strawberries and Yogurt. Mash 4 strawberries. Add 1 tablespoon plain yogurt. Mix well.

You may use a blender to mash strawberries and blend in the yogurt. But blend the ingredients at the lowest speed possible and only for a few seconds. You want a thick paste, not a liquid.

Variation: Instead of the strawberries, mash ½ cucumber in your blender. Mix with plain yogurt. It's very refreshing, especially if you let the mixture cool for a few minutes in the refrigerator before applying.

A real quickie: Simply place very thin slices of cucumber on your face while you lie down. Cucumber is a super astringent that will leave your face with a nice rosy look.

Yeast. Blend 1 packet of yeast with warm water until you have a thick paste.

Variation: Make it even richer and thicker by adding a teaspoon of honey to the yeast before adding the water.

Masks for normal to dry skin

Avocado. Peel one small avocado and cut it into small pieces. Place in a blender and mix for a few seconds on low speed until the mixture is creamy. Spread thickly on face. This fruit is rich in natural oils.

Variations: You may also mash the avocado with a fork and add a few drops of water. If your skin needs extra moisturing, throw in a few drops of your moisturizer instead of water.

Any leftovers? Shampoo your hair and work some of the avocado mixture into the lather before rinsing well. It's a terrific body builder.

Egg Yolk. Separate the white and the yolk of the egg. Beat the yolk with 1 tablespoon of olive oil or any vegetable oil.

Variation: You might like to add ½ tablespoon of honey to the yolk.

Honey. Mix honey with mashed avocado, or with fresh cream, or try it plain.

Yogurt. Try a coat of plain yogurt on your skin. It's very soothing. You could also mash a few pieces of banana into the yogurt before applying.

Oatmeal. Mix ¼ cup oatmeal with 1 tablespoon wheat germ, peanut, almond, sunflower, or safflower oil.

Variation: Instead of oatmeal, use cornmeal, bran, almond meal, or wheat germ instead.

Natural homemade cleansers

These kitchen cosmetics will help remove dead skin cells, clean out your pores, and stimulate your skin.

Mayonnaise is perfect for skin that's on the dry side. It contains egg yolks and vegetable oil, which are good for your skin. Use it as a cleanser or as a mask.

Cornmeal or **Oatmeal** are both gentle abrasives. Simply work up a lather on your face using your regular soap, then sprinkle the meal onto the palms of your hands. Scrub your face and neck with the mixture, using a light touch.

Avocado Peel and Lemon Peel are also slightly abrasive. Gently rub the avocado peel on your face if it's dry to normal, use the lemon peel if it's oily. You can also use both to smooth any rough, chapped spots on your elbows, feet, or hands.

Grapefruit Juice and Lemon Juice are naturally astringent. So if your skin is oily, put a few drops of either one into a sinkful of slightly cool water for a final rinse after you wash your face. Or, for a quick pickup, squeeze the juice of a lemon or grapefruit onto a cotton ball and pat your face lightly. It's even more refreshing if the juice is cool.

· FOUR ·

Acne: How to Fight Back

It's a skin problem that's so common among teens that some doctors consider it "normal," just part of growing up. But if you're plagued by acne, the fact that others are suffering too probably doesn't make you feel any better about your skin and the way you look. The old saying, "Misery loves company," doesn't seem to apply at all in this case. Even if you have only an occasional breakout, those few pimples that pop up when you aren't looking can cause you to feel ugly, angry, ashamed, depressed, different, and downright awful about yourself. It's a serious situation that calls for some immediate action: an all-out declaration of war on your zits.

Before you rush into your bathroom and launch a major attack on your pimples, you'd better get your facts straight. How well do you know your enemy? Washing your face ten times a day, for example, is a big waste of time and soap. Squeezing and picking at your pimples may release your anger but may also leave you with battle scars. Putting on a pound of makeup and spending another few dollars for yet another bottle of your favorite acne medication can give you a temporary feeling of victory, but you may still lose the war.

But don't give up. It isn't necessary to stay in your bedroom under the covers until you turn twenty-one, when your skin may clear up. Instead, fight back armed with the knowledge and know-how you need to get your acne under control. Here are straight answers to questions you might be too embarrassed to ask, or didn't think of asking, or asked before but want to ask again.

Q. *Why me?*
A. That's a very good question. Unfortunately, no one seems to have a very good answer for you. Medical researchers have pondered the problem for years, and still they don't know why some people are pimple-prone and others are not. They've concluded, therefore, that the tendency to develop acne is inherited, that it's all in the genes, just the way the color of your skin, hair, and eyes is determined. That's another way of saying *they don't know why you have pimples.* This doesn't mean that someday someone won't discover a miracle drug that wipes this mys-

terious affliction off the face of the earth. But until then you have to accept the fact that you were born with the gene for acne, and there's nothing you can do about it. You can, however, do something about your acne once you get it. Scientists haven't been idle. New treatments and techniques have been found that can control acne and one of them may work for you.

Q. *Does that mean I should see a doctor and get help?*
A. By all means. If your acne is getting worse, or if an occasional flare-up is getting you down, a visit to your family physician or a dermatologist (a skin doctor) is worth every penny. It could cost you anywhere from fifteen to fifty dollars, or more, to see a dermatologist, but keep in mind that your family's health insurance may cover the expense. And you may be spending more, right now, on cleansers and medications that you pick up on your own in the drug store.

A dermatologist will evaluate your skin condition and prescribe medication accordingly. There are new prescription drugs (drugs you can't buy without a doctor's prescription) being sold all the time, and most have proven to be very effective. Usually these medications cause the pimple to surface and the skin to peel while fighting bacteria at the same time. Or a doctor might give you an antibiotic, which fights the bacteria on your skin. In addition to medicine, a dermatologist may clean up your pores, extract blackheads and whiteheads using a special sterile instrument with a technique that doesn't cause skin to scar. Also, you'll get advice on what to use to care for your skin every day: special soaps, astringents, and makeup, for example. You'll also get a routine tailored to your particular needs.

Q. *Is it better to go to a dermatologist or a cosmetologist?*
A. If you've got a severe case of acne, you're better off seeing a dermatologist. Cosmetologists are not doctors and cannot prescribe medication, although often they will sell you their own astringents, peelers, cleansers, and makeup. These products probably won't make your acne worse, and may be very effective if you have only a mild case, but a doctor may decide you need more potent pimple-fighters.

A visit to a cosmetologist can cost anywhere from fifteen to fifty dollars, or more, and this is not covered by health insurance. Treatment consists of a facial: your skin might be steamed, the pores cleaned, blackheads and whiteheads removed using special instruments, and — after about an hour of this — a mask will probably be put on and then rinsed off. You will most likely feel terrific and your face will look fresh, rosy, and clean, so there are worse ways to spend your money. Why not ask your family doctor

or a dermatologist what he or she thinks? A
doctor might suggest you see a cosmetologist
once a month to help keep the problem under
control after he or she has done everything
possible to help you.

Q. *My face isn't dirty; I'm always washing
it! Why should a dermatologist or cosmetologist have to clean my skin for me?*
A. Don't be so defensive. Doctors may not
know how to cure acne, but they agree that
people do not get blemishes because they have
dirty, unwashed faces. This is a myth. Pimples are caused by a complicated chemical
process that goes on under your skin. Even
if you wash your face ten times a day, you're
not going to alter that process, and you may
even aggravate your acne with all that rubbing and scrubbing. Skin experts are knowl-
edgeable about skin cleansing. They use special instruments that you don't have at home
and wouldn't be able to use if you did. And
they can also give you tips on how to wash
properly. Your technique and cleanser may
not be doing any good and, in fact, could be
doing more harm than good. Just as there are
specialists in rug cleaning, engine cleaning,
typewriter cleaning, and house cleaning,
there are people who make a living at skin
cleaning. It pays to get their advice and as-
sistance. Consider this: you may not have
excessively oily skin! Improper cleansing can

cause pimples on dry, sensitive, and even perfectly normal skin.

Q. *If dirt doesn't cause acne, what exactly does? How do you get a pimple?*
A. This is probably a more detailed explanation than you want, but remember, it's important to get your facts straight or you'll go around fighting the wrong enemy.

Most people get pimples when they enter their teen years because at this time the body begins to produce increased amounts of hormones. One of these hormones is called androgen. It's the male sex hormone (which is why more men have acne than women), but all females produce androgen, too. What androgen does, for some reason, is enlarge and rev up the sebaceous (oil) glands that are attached to the hair follicles (small canals all over your body that produce hair). Although you've got hair follicles everywhere, there are more and larger hair follicles on your face, neck, back, and shoulders, all the spots where acne strikes.

Once the oil glands get going, they give off a fatty substance called sebum. The sebum has nowhere to go but up and out of the canal, flowing onto your skin, resulting in oilier skin during your teens. While the sebum is traveling through the follicle, on its way out, it usually picks up scales, or dead skin cells, from the walls of the follicle, and sometimes bacteria that's hanging around as well.

So now you have oil, dead skin cells, and bacteria in the follicles and on your face. Once this unappetizing mixture is allowed to sit in your pores for a while it may dry out and darken, causing a blackhead. As you can see, they are not caused by dirt. Everyone has bacteria wandering around in their follicles; everyone has some oil on their face; and dead skin cells are extremely common. Just why they get together and form a pimple is really a big mystery. But doctors do know that when the follicle becomes so stuffed with this mixture, a chemical reaction occurs, and a pimple is formed.

So you can be squeaky clean yet still have acne. However, it could be that your cleanser is not dissolving the oil on your face, so you get a greasy build-up, a perfect environment for pimples to breed. And oily skin can look as flaky as dry skin. Maybe an abrasive cleanser will slough them off. A skin care specialist can give you just the right cleansers and tell you just how to use them so they are most effective.

Q. *Is there a right way to wash your face? And with what?*

A. Most experts recommend that you wash your face two or three times a day and follow with an astringent (see Chapter 2 on skin cleansing), such as alcohol or witch hazel. There are many medicated acne soaps and cleansers at your pharmacy that help dissolve excess oil, slough off dead skin cells, and reduce the bacterial population on your skin. Experiment until you find the one that works on your skin. Try one for two weeks. (It takes at least that long before you'll begin to see results.) If you see no improvement, switch to another. You might also have better results if you alternate between two or three cleansers, washing with a different one every week. The same rules apply to any acne medication.

Experts also believe that it's best to shampoo your hair every day, if possible, especially if it touches your face. Oily skin usually goes along with oily hair, and you already have more oil on your face than you need.

If you wear makeup, make sure it's water-based. Some are even medicated. And there are acne medications that are flesh-colored and act as a cover-up. Stay away from heavy moisturizers and cleansing creams. More on makeup, coming up in Chapter 8.

Q. *My parents say I don't eat or sleep right and that's why I have acne. Is that true?*
A. For the most part, untrue. Stop blaming yourself for your acne! And remind your parents that it's inherited.

New research has shown that sweets, chocolate, potato chips, cola drinks, pizza, fried foods, and shellfish do not cause acne. Only in rare cases do these foods trigger a breakout. Of course, you could be one of those rare birds who is allergic, or particularly sensitive, to one of these treats. So if you find that each bar of chocolate you consume leads to five new pimples, then *stop*! But keep in mind that the problem may not be the chocolate bar but the fact that you aren't getting enough of the foods you need to have a well-balanced diet. So do try to eat your share of good-for-you foods.

Sleep, too much or too little, is also not the culprit. Everyone needs a different amount of sleep at different times of their lives. Of course, if you really don't get enough sleep you probably feel tired most of the time, and your entire system may be out of whack. You could be putting yourself under unnecessary pressure, and stress is not good for your skin. When you feel rested, your entire body functions more smoothly.

Do they say you sleep too much? Well, ask yourself if you doze off because you're tired or because you're depressed. If it's depression and sleep is your escape, then try to come up for air once in a while — you might find something that would be more fun to do. Exercise is a good pick-me-up. If you can't exercise for twenty minutes a day, then take up a sport you might like or walk around the block ten times. A better attitude and better skin might be the payoff. Once again, it's common sense: a smooth-running body is the key to fitness, so you must get the parts moving once in a while. And your skin is a living part of your body, not the wrapping.

You'll find much more on food and exercise for your skin's sake in the next chapter.

Q. *I do break out occasionally, but I don't think it's food or sleep. What could it be?*
A. Emotional stress can do it. You can worry a pimple into being. Hot, humid weather is the perfect environment for developing pimples. And many women break out before, during or after their menstrual period; that's when hormones act up the most. You can't do anything about the weather or menstruation, but you can try to tackle the problems that are making you tense. Calm down, cool off, and think of how good that will be for your skin. Try to work out your tensions by exercising — your body and your mouth. Talk to someone. You'll be surprised how powerful just a good talk is.

Q. *Will my acne last forever?*
A. Odds are it will be all over by the time you're twenty-one. But just how long it stays and exactly when it will disappear can't be predicted. In two months, two years, or five years your face may clear up. You may see a dermatologist for one visit or fourteen, or you may be able to get your acne under control on your own. But acne very, very rarely lasts forever.

Q. *Will I be scarred for life?*

A. Definitely not, if you stop squeezing and picking at the little monsters. Itchy fingers can make a so-so pimple a real stunner by spreading the oil and bacteria around. If you simply can't stand looking in the mirror, sit down with a dermatologist or cosmetologist and let a pro do the pinching and probing for you.

The war against acne may be a tough and bitter one, but you can win. Fight back!

· FIVE ·

Work Wonders From the Inside Out

Your skin care routine may be perfect. Your cleanser, moisturizer, and makeup may be exactly what your skin type calls for. But all this, although a giant step in the right direction, is not enough. For skin to look healthy, it has to *be* healthy, and the only way to achieve that goal is from the inside out.

It isn't a very difficult goal. All you have to do are two good things for yourself:

1. **Start eating for your skin's sake.** Now that you know what to put *on* your skin, you have to turn your attention to what you take *in* to nourish it. Like every other part of your body, your skin needs the nutrients it can only get from food. Change your eating habits, and you'll see a difference in your skin.

2. Start exercising for your skin's sake.
Take twenty minutes a day to really get your
body moving, your muscles stretching and
working, and your circulation revved up. The
increased activity and circulation is guaran-
teed to give you healthier-looking skin. Of
course, there are other advantages to daily
exercise: you'll firm up your flabby muscles
and get a shapelier body, and you'll also feel
a whole lot more energetic.

Beauty foods

Relax. You're not going to get a lecture on
the evils of chocolate. In fact, experts now
agree that food such as chocolate and pizza,
don't necessarily lead to breakouts. If your
skin flares up after eating chocolate, it could
be because you've over-indulged. Too much
of anything can be bad for you. Or perhaps
your skin is allergic or sensitive to a particular food at this time in your life. Too much
cheese, or just one single morsel, for example,
gives some rare individuals pimples.

In general, nutritionists believe that if
your skin breaks out after eating chocolate,
it is probably because there is simply too
much of it and other sweets in your diet and
not nearly enough of the foods your skin
craves and needs. Does that mean there are
certain foods that will magically wipe out
your acne? Is there one vitamin that will
make your skin glow? The answer is a defi-

nite *no*. But there are foods that will keep your skin, and every inch of you, healthy. Do you know if you're getting your fair share of skin foods? To find out, take this test:

Make a list of exactly what you ate yesterday, the day before that, and the day before that, too. Include all meals and all snacks. Now update the list to include everything you've eaten so far today and keep up the list until you have a full five days of menus.

Once your list is complete, answer these six questions:

1. Did you have at least two servings of a dairy product every day?

The following items equal *one* serving each: 1 cup (8 oz.) skim or whole milk; 1 malt (8 oz.); 1 oz. cheese (American, cheddar, Edam, Swiss); 4 oz. ice cream (2 or 3 scoops); 1 carton yogurt (8 oz.); ½ cup cottage cheese.

2. Did you have at least two or more servings a day of a high-protein food?

These are foods such as meat (beef, veal, lamb, pork), fish, and poultry (about 3 oz. to a serving); eggs; dried beans; peas; lentils; peanut butter; some nuts.

The following items equal one serving each: 3 oz. hamburger meat; 1 frankfurter; 3 oz. pork chop; 2 eggs; 3 oz. sandwich meat (bologna, salami); 1 slice pizza; 3 oz. tuna fish; 1 cup lentils or beans; ¼ cup dry roasted peanuts; 2 tablespoons peanut butter; 1 oz.

cheese (you cannot count cheese in this group if you've used it to meet your daily requirement in the dairy group).

3. Did you have at least one serving a day of a citrus fruit or juice, or any fruit or juice high in vitamin C?

The following items equal one serving each: 6 oz. orange, tomato, or unsweetened grapefruit juice; ½ grapefruit or cantaloupe; ½ cup stewed tomatoes; 1 med. size orange or tangerine; 1 cup strawberries.

4. Did you have at least three servings a day of vegetables and/or other fruits not listed in Question 3? Was at least one of the three servings either a deep yellow or dark green vegetable, such as spinach, broccoli, carrots, sweet potatoes?

The following items equal one serving each: ½ cup raw or cooked vegetable or fruit; 1 banana, apple, pear, or peach; ½ cup sauerkraut; ½ cup corn or peas; 1 boiled potato.

5. Did you have at least four servings of bread or cereal every day?

The following items equal one serving each: 1 slice of bread; ½ to ¾ cup cooked cereal, cornmeal, grits, pasta, or rice; 1 muffin or biscuit; 1 hamburger or frankfurter roll.

6. Did you have at least 2 tablespoons of a fat or oil every day?

This can be, butter, margarine, salad oil, or mayonnaise.

A perfect score means that your diet is perfectly balanced. You're getting just what you need to keep your body — and, of course, your skin — healthy. Another plus: you feel alive and healthy all the time.

But if your daily diet is far from perfect or could stand improvement, chances are your skin shows the lack. Feed your skin the nutrients that are so essential for its health, and it will pay you back.

The top skin snacks

Give your daily diet a nutritional boost by snacking on foods that not only taste good, but are good for you, too. Your skin will love these wholesome snacks, and so will you.

1. **Break for yogurt.** Be sure to pick a brand that contains no sugar or additives but does contain live bacilli — ingredients are listed right on the label. If you're not crazy about plain yogurt then doctor it up — try different ways to fix it so you like it. For example: Mix a few tablespoons of yogurt with a teaspoon of honey and put a dollop over any chilled fruit. (More yogurt recipes coming up.)

2. **Pop a strawberry.** Stock up on them when they're in season and pop one whenever

you need a lift. They're naturally sweet and an excellent source of vitamin C. Here's a recipe that will make your mouth water: Mix 1 cup of ripe strawberries with ½ cup of yogurt and freeze. It's just like ice cream! Or make your own strawberry yogurt: Crush a few strawberries, add a couple of teaspoons of honey, and pour the mixture over a bowl of plain yogurt, or even ice cream.

3. **Have a crunchy munch.** Oats are not for breakfast only. Here's how to make a nutty-tasting oat topping to sprinkle over ice cream, yogurt, fruits, and puddings. Ingredients: 1¼ cup oat cereal, uncooked; ⅓ cup firmly packed brown sugar; ⅓ cup butter or margarine, melted; ⅓ cup chopped nuts; ¼ teaspoon cinnamon. Mix all the ingredients together in a large bowl. Cook the mixture in a skillet over medium heat, stirring constantly, until it is a golden brown. Sprinkle it all on an ungreased cookie sheet to cool. Then just store it in your refrigerator in a tightly covered container. The recipe makes about two cups that will keep for up to three months.

4. **Nibble on a carrot.** Whenever you get a strong desire to chew on something, remember nothing is more chewable than the carrot. Keep one in a plastic bag in your pocketbook for an emergency snack. Buy carrots with no bumps or blemishes, scrub them with a vegetable brush under running water (never peel

carrots), and store them in the fridge, where they'll keep for two weeks. The smaller the carrot, the sweeter it is.

5. **Eat sweet potatoes year round.** At midday or whenever your stomach craves something substantial, bake yourself a sweet potato or a yam. They're both chock-full of vitamins A and C. Just bake it, with the skin on, in a 350°F. oven for one hour. You could bake it with butter or margarine, if you like, and for extra sweetness, sprinkle on cinnamon, too. And do eat the whole thing — many of the nutrients are locked in the skin of the potato.

6. **Stock up on seeds, nuts and raisins.** Always keep a bag full of your favorite nuts on hand. Almonds and walnuts are particularly rich in nutrients. Add them to breads and cookies that you bake; sprinkle some over ice cream; try them in vegetable dishes to add crunch and taste. Sunflower seeds are another smart snack. Keep a bowl of them within easy reach as you do homework or watch T.V. They're packed with protein. Mix different kinds of nuts with sunflower seeds, raisins, and other dried fruit for a combination that can't be beat.

7. **Say cheese anytime.** Have a chunk or slice of your favorite cheese a few times a day. Make grilled cheese sandwiches anytime, using American, Swiss, or mozzarella.

Or grill cheese on plain crackers. Have you ever tried English muffin pizza? Just split the muffin in two, smooth on prepared tomato sauce, add chopped mozzarella (whole or skimmed), salt, pepper, and oregano. Broil until cheese is slightly brown on top.

8. **Slice an avocado.** A real skin food, avocados are available year round. Buy one when it's ripe, which means it's slightly soft to the touch, and it will keep in the fridge for about a week. For a taste treat, prepare an avocado salad: Put a few slices on a bed of lettuce leaves, drizzle lemon juice and olive oil on top, and salt and pepper to taste.

Workouts that put a glow on

You can rev up your circulation, give your complexion a rosy, healthy glow, and get your body in shape at the same time. You can do it all merely by exercising every day for twenty minutes. Why not give it a try? For the next three weeks, resolve to work out every day. At the end of that time, you will no doubt see and feel the difference.

What sort of exercise should you be doing? You have three alternatives; choose the one that you think you'll enjoy most because, above all, your workout must be fun. If it isn't, chances are you'll drop the activity before the three weeks are up. Here are your choices:

An at-home exercise program

You probably know how to do plenty of exercises — sit-ups, toe-touchers, head or shoulder stands, waist twists, push-ups, and such. So set a timer for twenty minutes and do them all. The best time to work out is in the morning, when you're feeling fresh and ready for anything. But any time of day will do, as long as it's always the same time. A regular schedule will help you make exercising every day a habit. Important: Be sure to wait at least two hours after you've eaten.

A few hints to help you along: Always wear an outfit that allows you to move comfortably. And *do* work out to music. Experiment until you find the perfect beat, one that suits your pace. You'll be surprised how good this sort of daily routine is going to be for your morale. Finally, if you find that your workout doesn't work up a sweat, then it wasn't strenuous enough. So add a few challenging exercises, ones that force you to push yourself a little beyond what is easy and comfortable.

At-home rhythmetrics

If all the usual exercises bore you, then try something different: Move to music. Every day, or whenever you need a change from your regular routine, dance and jump rope to any sounds that turn you on. Start by jumping rope for three to four minutes and then, when you're ready, just dance. What could be more fun?

Any rope will do. You can jump in place or jump around the house. The only requirement is a good pair of sneakers. As for the dancing, anything goes. Relax. No one is watching. Really exaggerate your movements. Pretend you're on stage. Unless you're prespiring, you're not dancing fast enough. And here's a bonus: You'll burn up plenty of calories.

Go out and play

Take up a sport. There must be one you'd like to try. How about swimming, or handball, volleyball, softball, bowling, soccer, basketball, bicycling, racquetball, squash, jogging, speedwalking, or bowling? Whatever you choose, go all out. Decide to get really good at one sport. Set yourself goals: five miles of cycling, three sets of tennis, five laps in the pool, an hour of racquetball. Learn all you can about the sport — the more you know, the more interesting it will be to you. So get a good book on swimming or jogging, for example. Enter tournaments; join a team. The challenge and the competition will spur you on. And when fitness is your major goal, you can't lose.

· SIX ·

Love Your Skin All Over

Why stop at your neck? What about the skin from your chin on down? If your shoulders, arms, elbows, back, legs, and feet are not as soft, smooth, and clear as you like, then the problem is that you've been neglecting ninety percent of your body. The solution is a cinch: the total body skincare program coming up. It's complete, but you'll find it isn't very complicated or terribly time-consuming. And the time you spend on your skin all over will probably be the most relaxing, refreshing, satisfying beauty break you'll take all day.

Once you get to know a few quick tricks, and get into a few good habits, your total skin care program will become second nature to you, as automatic as brushing your teeth. All the how-tos you need are here, and basic to each one is the most natural beautifier, cleanser, and skin conditioner on earth: water. It's the key element in your total body treatment: plain ordinary water, straight from the tap. Let it work its wonders for you, from your neck to your toes, starting with the water in your bath.

The bath

Make it warm and wonderful

A short shower or a five-minute soak in the tub should, of course, be part of your daily cleansing routine. Not only isn't it unnecessary for cleansing purposes to linger any longer than it takes to soap up and rinse off, long showers and baths are surprisingly hard on your skin. All that soap and water is drying because it washes away surface oils that lock in the moisture your skin needs to stay soft and smooth.

But once a week, you ought to find the time for a long, warm bath. The difference: This bath is skin-conditioning. In only twenty minutes, you'll deep-clean and soften your skin, get rid of rough dry spots and flakes. An added bonus: You'll feel recharged and good all over.

Before you step into your tub, however, you'll need:

• *Brushes.* A long-handled back brush and one for your nails and feet.

• *Sponges*. Get a couple of natural sponges that come right from the sea — a large and a small one.

• *A Loofah*. It's a rough, dried gourd that swells and softens somewhat in water (you might like the kind that has terry cloth on one side). It's great for giving yourself a rubdown, revving up your circulation, removing dead skin cells, and making your skin gleam.

• *A Pumice Stone*. It's a small piece of hardened lava that's ideal for buffing and smoothing rough spots on the soles and heels of your feet.

• *Soap*. Not any old soap will do. Be sure to match your soap to your skin type. There are bath soaps for dry, oily, sensitive, and normal skin. The rule is: Don't use a soap on your body that would be too harsh to use on your face.

Your bath water should be the same temperature as your body: 98.6°F. If you're used to hot baths this may feel a bit cool to you, so keep your bathroom warm and cozy by closing any doors and windows while the water is running and during your soak.

Before you begin, put a few drops of baby or bath oil in the palms of your hands and massage it on to the dry, bumpy, rough areas of your body: your elbows, feet, knees, and any other spots that look particularly dry. If your skin seems dry and flaky and feels taut all over, then put a few drops of oil in your bath water, too.

Now slip into the water and let your body go limp. Rest your head on a towel or bath pillow. You might like to do a few de-tensing exercises while you sit there: Roll your neck and shoulders and roll your ankles around in large circles. Then try to relax every muscle.

Bath time is also a good time to deep-condition your hair: The steam will help the moisturizers in the conditioner to penetrate. And massage your scalp while you're at it. You could also put on a facial mask and even pluck you're eyebrows while you soak.

Finally, when you're totally relaxed, get down to some deep skin cleansing. With a soapy sponge, using small circular motions, rub your entire body, working up a rich lather. Then, with your loofah, take long, firm strokes on your shoulders, arms, legs, and feet. Then use a pumice on your water-softened heels and soles to get them smooth as can be. Finally, take your long-handled brush and give your back a brisk once over.

When you're all through, pat yourself dry with a soft towel and while your body is still a bit damp slather on your moisturizer. You can use your regular moisturizer or any body or hand cream or lotion. You might like to finish off with a light dusting of powder or talc — very refreshing in warm weather — and then even a splash of after-bath fragrance.

Make it cool and refreshing

Any time you want an invigorating, stimulating soak, fill your tub with cool water: under 75°F. It's an especially nice thing to do for yourself when the weather is warm or after you've been exercising strenuously and your skin is perspiring and greasy. You'll close your pores, give your skin tone a lift, and get your energy up again.

No matter how warm you feel, never allow the water to get icy cold. In fact, you might even want to invest in a small, inexpensive bath thermometer. And never soak in cool water for more than three or four minutes.

If you can't get yourself to step into cool water, here's a trick: Start by sitting in a tub of warm water then turn on the tap and allow cool water to trickle in, gradually lowering the temperature. That way, your body has a chance to get accustomed to the cold. Another plus: The sound of running water is very soothing and relaxing.

After a cool bath, don't forget your body moisturizer. Slather it on all over while your skin is still damp.

Make it hot and super-soothing

When your muscles are aching and tired, when you need help getting to sleep, there's nothing better than soaking in a tub filled with hot (higher than your body temperature) water for twenty minutes — never any longer. Your heart will beat a bit faster, your breathing will be more shallow, and you'll feel somewhat drained of energy: Plan on just sitting around or taking a nap afterwards.

Never plunge your body into hot water. Sneak in, one small step at a time. Once you've grown accustomed to the temperature, use your sponges and loofah to massage your sore muscles and tone your skin, sloughing off any dirty, greasy, flaky surface cells.

To finish, quickly rinse yourself off under a cool shower or allow some cool water to trickle into the tub in order to get your body temperature back to normal. You might even give yourself an alcohol rub, or use a refreshing after-bath splash after you towel-dry. Finally, moisturize your skin all over while your body is still damp. Then wrap up in a big towel or cozy bathrobe and relax for an hour.

The shower

Make it a stimulating experience

This shower is a real eye-opener in the morning. You'll step out of it with your skin looking rosier. The trick: Simply keep switching from hot to cold water for about ten minutes, first a few minutes of hot, a minute of cold, back to hot, then cold again. This will quickly open and close your pores

and rev up your circulation. If you have a
shower massage attachment, all the better.
The pulsating jets of water are very invigorating ˙and muscle-relaxing. Afterwards,
don't forget your body moisturizer.

Special treatments for special problems

Is your back blemished, are your elbows
gray and bumpy, your legs ashen and flaky?
Or maybe your feet are callused, your soles
tough and peeling. Take a look at your arms
and shoulders. Has a fading tan left them
looking blotchy? Here's how to take care of
these special problems and others. Each
remedy calls for some extra time and effort
but the results are worth it, and you'll get
into some smart beauty habits.

Banish back blemishes

You can clear up the skin on your back and
shoulders, although you may have to stretch
your arm muscles a bit to do it. The first
step: Once a week, in your bath or shower,
use a medicated, abrasive cleanser on these
areas. Just put a little of the grainy cream
on your loofah or your long-handled back
brush and scrub your back and shoulders
gently. Rinse in warm, then cool water.
Gently pat yourself dry, then dab the blemishes with a cotton ball soaked in your as-

tringent, rubbing alcohol, or witch hazel. The second step: Each time you shower or bathe, sponge down your back and shoulders using a medicated soap or cleanser. Follow with an astringent every time.

Turn rough spots silky

You should, of course, be using your loofah (on your elbows, knees, legs, and feet) and a pumice stone (on your heels and soles) at least once a week. But once in a while those areas need extra attention.

The Salt Massage. To get rid of the flakes, mix up a paste of sea salt or plain coarse salt and warm water in a cup. Then sit on the edge of the tub and massage any rough spots with the mixture, making small circular motions with your fingers or a washcloth. Now step into a warm or cool bath or shower and rinse off. If your skin is dry and flaky all over, pour a few handfuls of salt in your bath water and sponge down your entire body. When you're through, slather on the moisturizer.

The Grainy Shower. Before you go under the spray, prepare this creamy abrasive: Blend ½ cup of oatmeal with one-half a small jar of cold cream. While you're standing in the shower, before you turn on the tap, massage your elbows, heels, knees, and shoulders with the mixture. It's terrific for gently rubbing away the layer of dead skin that causes discoloration and blotchiness. Finally, rinse off in warm water, then cool, and moisturize while your skin is still wet.

The Elbow Whitener and Softener. It's the old lemon trick and it really works! Cut a lemon in half and give each of your elbows a cool rubdown. Next, while sitting at a table, bend your arms and cap each elbow with a lemon half for fifteen minutes. Then rub the heels of your feet with the lemon halves to whiten and soften them, too. Rinse well and moisturize.

The Foot Bath. Fill up a basin with sea salt and water and then scrub your feet while they're soaking, using your small nail brush. Tackle really rough spots with the pumice stone. It's a good time to prepare your nails for a pedicure, too. While your cuticles are water-softened, push them back using an orange stick.

Or, before you shower, mix up a paste of oatmeal and warm water and then, using your small manicure brush, scrub the rough spots with the grainy mixture.

Did you know that any mask you can use on your face can also be used on your feet? So next time you give yourself a facial, give your feet the same special treatment.

Always dry your feet well, especially between the toes, to prevent flaking and peeling. And be sure to finish off with your body moisturizer. In warm weather when your feet perspire, or in cold weather when you've worn boots all day long, it's a good idea to dust on foot powder to keep your feet smelling sweet and looking smooth.

The Leg Gleamers. If the skin on your thighs and calves could be lovelier, smoother, softer, and shinier, your problem is dry skin. So before you take a bath or shower, make it a rule to always rub on baby or bath oil. It's not enough to throw a few drops of oil in your bath water, because most of it will just float on top or cling to the sides of the tub, never reaching your legs. And it's also important to end with a cool rinse to close the pores. Finish by moisturizing your legs while they're still damp. This technique locks in the moisture by replacing the natural oils that have been washed down the drain.

Dry skin here could also be caused by incorrect hair removal techniques. Here are a few tips to help you do it the right way.

• *Shaving with a razor.* Use one that's lightweight, easy to grip, and designed just for women. Always be certain the blade is sharp and clean, because a dull one can irritate your skin and lead to nicks. It's also necessary to rinse off the blade after every stroke to prevent nicks and get a smoother shave. Always use a lubricant, a shaving lotion or cream or lots of soap, and warm water. This softens the hair, making it easier to remove. For a silkier finish, work against the direction of hair growth, gently moving the razor up the leg. Be extra careful around such trouble spots as the ankles and shins. If you get a nick, don't panic: Apply pressure with a wet cotton ball. Rinse and pat dry gently, then moisturize.

If you only have a slight fuzz on your thighs, why shave there at all? You can make your facial, arm, and this leg hair much less visible by bleaching it. Buy a facial bleach and give yourself a patch test first, the day before. If your hair is especially dark, you have to bleach it twice, but do wait a day before you bleach again. Follow the directions carefully, of course.

• *Shaving with an electric shaver.* You may not get as close a shave with an electric, and you may have to shave more often, but it's kinder to your skin than a regular razor. Be sure your skin is very dry, never damp, or use a pre-shave lotion. And, of course, never take your electric shaver into the bath or shower. For a smoother finish, take short strokes and don't forget to moisturize afterwards. If an electric shave is not close enough for you, use a regular razor every other time you shave.

• *Using a hair-dissolving depilatory.* Painless but potent, depilatories contain chemicals that are strong enough to dissolve hair but gentle enough to use on your legs, underarms, and sometimes even on your face. So read the package directions carefully. Your skin may be sensitive to the chemicals, so make sure to do the patch test as directed. Follow with a shower to remove every trace of the substance.

• *Waxing away hair.* There are at-home waxing kits now available. You can also have waxing done professionally. The minus: It's slightly painful. The plus: It only takes a few minutes and lasts four to six weeks. You might consider waxing during the summer when you probably shave your legs more often. All that shaving, in addition to the effects of the sun, salt water, and chlorine, can be extremely drying — so don't forget to moisturize.

• SEVEN •

Sun-Kissed Skin Care

Summer's the time when you want a fabulous, healthy-looking color and a radiance only the sun can give you. You want a glorious tan — not a red, raw burn — and you want that tanned skin to look smooth and golden, not parched and blotchy. It's very easy to overdo and spend too much time in the sun. Too much of even a good thing like the sun can be damaging to your skin, no matter how readily you tan. Couple overexposure to the sun with the normal summertime exposure to salt water, chlorine, and heat — all of which are drying — and you've got problem skin. And that's not at all what you wanted when you set out for the beach or your backyard.

So be a reasonable sunbather. This doesn't mean staying indoors or hiding under a beach umbrella or a big sun hat all summer long.

That would be unreasonable, probably impossible, and even unhealthy, because some sun is good for you. The sun may help clear up your complexion, for example; and it's essential for the natural formation of vitamin D, necessary for building strong bones and teeth. But keep in mind that a tan is actually a protective reaction to injury: The sun is the culprit and your skin is the victim.

The process of tanning itself is part of your body's defense system. Here's how it works: The outer layer of your skin, the epidermis, contains cells that produce pigment, a protein called melanin. The more melanin you have naturally (that you are born with) the darker your skin and hair color and, usually, the less sensitive you are to sunlight. When exposed to the sun's ultraviolet rays, which comprise just one percent of all the sun's rays that reach the earth, melanin darkens and so you tan. Melanin darkens in order to reflect, scatter, and absorb the sun's rays. If it didn't, your skin would be injured — in other words, you'd burn. A sunburn is as real as any other kind of burn, and tanning is simply a self-defense mechanism, something your body does involuntarily, not unlike the blink of an eye.

You may have quite a few misconceptions about the sun and tanning, and maybe that's why you burn and never get the wonderful tan you're after. To avoid that painful experience and disappointment, here are some myths — and truths — you ought to get straight in your mind.

Myth: You can get a good tan in a day.

It may be a tan but it's definitely not a good one. The best-looking, longest-lasting tan is one that you get gradually. It takes time, days at least, for melanin to darken. Unless you give it a chance to do its job, you'll merely burn, if not the first day, then the second or third.

Myth: You can't burn in the shade.

Although hats, umbrellas, and trees offer some protection, only half the sun's rays are stopped. They can even penetrate clothing. And rays are reflected off the sand, water, and shiny objects, which means they bounce off these things and reach you. So whenever you're in the sun, a sunscreen preparation is a must, even if it's a cloudy day. The sun may be hiding, but about fifty percent or more of its burning rays can still get through to you, so beware.

Myth: You can't burn while you're in the water.

Not only will the exposed areas of your skin burn, but the rays can penetrate water. Water also reflects rays, making them even stronger. Always reapply your sunscreen right after your dip, because the water probably washed most of it away.

Myth: *Wear a cover-up and you won't burn.*

Yes, the sun still gets through to you, even if you're covered up. And don't think they'll be stopped by a wet T-shirt either. Cover-ups do, however, offer some protection, especially if the fabric is tightly woven and dark in color.

Myth: *Keep moving and you won't burn.*

The sun will follow you, no matter how fast you run. You need the protection of a sunscreen even more, in fact, because when you're standing up, particularly sensitive areas are exposed to the sun: the tops of your shoulders and feet, your nose, ears, scalp (it can burn, too), and the backs of your knees.

Myth: *Sunscreen preparations can increase your tan.*

What they really do is *allow* you to tan by letting the melanin build up gradually and prevent a bad burn. Nothing in the preparation itself, other than the screen, promotes tanning, unless it contains a skin-staining ingredient.

Myth: *Put on a sunscreen in the morning and you're safe all day.*

Once is not enough. Every few hours, you must reapply your sunscreen. Even if your skin is naturally dark, and even if you never even go near the water, perspiration and contact with towels and clothing removes some of the screen. And the screen can't do its job unless it's on your skin.

Myth: Oil your body and you'll tan faster.

Actually, you'll probably burn faster, unless your skin is completely insensitive to the sun (which is very rare). Substances such as baby oil, coconut oil, and cocoa butter may prevent your skin from drying out but offer little or no protection, because they do not contain any sunscreen at all.

Myth: If you're black you won't burn.

Your skin does contain a large amount of melanin, depending of course on how dark it is, but you too can burn. Not only that, your skin could take on a blotchy, uneven color. So you should also use a sunscreen, one that's mild and soothing.

What's your sun type?

Before you can select the proper sunscreen for your skin, one that offers you the protection you need and allows you to tan as well, you must know your sun type. Your sun type is not the same as your skin type but, instead, indicates your skin's sensitivity to the sun. The more sun-sensitive your skin, the more likely you'll burn, and the stronger your sunscreen should be.

Now you can tell exactly how potent your sunscreen is simply by reading the label. Every sun preparation must list its SPF, or Sun Protection Factor (it's the law). The SPF is a number from 2 (minimal protection) to 15 (maximum protection). That means if your skin is the type that can stay in the sun unprotected for only ten minutes without burning, and you choose a sunscreen with an SPF of 2, you can stay in the sun twice as long: twenty minutes. Naturally, you should choose a stronger sunscreen, one with a higher SPF, if you intend to sun longer than twenty minutes.

To determine your sun type, check the color of the skin on your body that hasn't been exposed to the sun very often, your breasts, back, and legs, for example. Then read on and find the category that best describes your coloring.

TYPE A. Most likely your skin is light in color, you have blue eyes, red or blond hair, and you may freckle. Your hair may be darker and your eyes on the green side, but you would describe yourself as fair. You burn easily, almost never tan, and really can't stay in the sun longer than twenty minutes without turning bright red.

Your SPF: 8 to 15 is best.

TYPE B. You're fair, too, with light or dark hair and light eyes. You also burn very easily but eventually you tan, although not very much. After twenty minutes in the noonday sun, your skin is red, or at least an uncomfortable-looking pink.

Your SPF: 6 to 7 will keep you protected.

TYPE C. Your hair is on the dark side, as are your eyes. Your skin isn't fair nor is it dark, but somewhere in the middle range. You burn a little, you tan slowly, but over a period of time you do end up with a deep color. Your skin is within the normal range.

Your SPF: 4 to 5 is all you need.

TYPE D. Your hair is dark, your eyes are dark, and your skin is not at all sensitive to the sun. In fact, you can soak in the hot sun for thirty minutes to half an hour and not burn at all. You tan very easily, and although you have had burns they have been very slight and have disappeared quickly.

Your SPF: 2 to 3, which is the least amount of protection.

Any sunscreen you buy contains chemicals that filter out ultraviolet rays, allowing you to tan rather than burn. Choose a cream, gel, or lotion, whichever one feels most soothing on your skin and leaves it feeling softest. The most common chemical ingredient is PABA (para-aminobenzoic acid), and it's usually found in preparations containing alcohol. If these sunscreens irritate your skin, you may be allergic to PABA or the alcohol may. be too drying for you. In that case, ask your pharmacist for a sunscreen with a different chemical base or one that doesn't contain alcohol.

Sunblocks, also called sun shades, contain filtering chemicals, too, but these ingredients are opaque so that they almost completely block out or reflect the sun's burning rays. It's wise to use a sunblock on your nose and lips if they're super-sensitive to the sun or if you must be out in the sun for a long period of time, when you're sailing, for example, or working as a life guard.

Whatever sunscreen or sunblock you choose, read the label and follow the directions carefully. Some must be applied one or two hours before you go into the sun and some have a cumulative effect, which means the more you use them the more effective they become, because the chmicals build up on your skin.

How to tan

There's a science to it, a foolproof method that will give you your best tan ever. All you need is self-discipline.

• *Start slowly.* A tan built up over weeks of exposure lasts longer and looks better. So, the first day stay in the sun for only fifteen minutes, using a sunscreen with an SPF one number higher than recommended for your sun type. The next day stay another fifteen minutes. Finally try half an hour. If you burn, skip a day or two. Never stay out for more than thirty minutes the first few times you go sun bathing.

• *Once you have a slight tan,* you can switch to a sunscreen with a lower SPF. If weeks go by and you haven't been sunbathing, start all over with the higher SPF preparation. Don't take any chances. A burn is painful and not very pretty to look at. And once you peel, you're back to square one and have to begin building up your tan again from scratch.

• *After any stretch of time in the sun,* even just fifteen minutes, apply a moisturizer or after-sun lotion or cream to prevent flaking and peeling.

Sun dos and don'ts

DO use a sunscreen on your lips — they can burn, too. Now you can even get lip colors with sunscreens added.

DON'T put on perfume or cologne, and don't wash with deodorant soap, before going into the sun. The chemicals in fragrances and in deodorant soaps make some skin types even more sun-sensitive than usual and can cause a rash or allergic reaction. And, if you're on any sort of medication, check with your doctor because it, too, can increase your sensitivity to the sun.

DON'T use a reflector. Those foil gadgets that reflect the sun's rays increase your chances of burning, even if you already have a tan.

DON'T stop using a sunscreen once you've tanned. It's possible to burn even on top of a very deep tan, although it does reduce the penetration of ultra-violet rays. Instead, switch to a sunscreen with a lower SPF because you need less protection.

DO change your makeup once you've got a tan. Pale makeup may look fine during the winter but only looks pasty white on top of your sun-kissed skin. And if you're going to be outdoors in the sun but must wear makeup, do try to find foundation, eye shadow and lipstick that contain sunscreens.

First aid for burns

Okay, so you blew it. You stayed in the sun too long and now you're lobster red, your skin feels taut and itchy, your head feels hot, and every inch of you feels as if it's on fire. *If you also have blisters and feel nauseous or dizzy, see a doctor at once.* But if what you have is an awful but run-of-the-mill sunburn, here's how to cool it.

• *Take a sun bath.* Not in the sun, of course, but in a tub filled with warm water — never hot or icy cold water, but a bit cooler than your body temperature. Before you step in, add a cup of cider vinegar or bicarbonate of soda, which will take out the sting and itchiness and leave you feeling more comfortable for a while.

• *Try cool compresses.* Soak a soft washcloth in cool skim milk and apply it to your most sensitive areas. Don't reach for ice packs. They sound like a good solution, but they don't work.

• *Moisturize all over.* Don't use anything that's very greasy or feels tight on your skin after it has dried. Just a light moisturizer or after-sun lotion or cream is enough, followed by a light dusting with talcum powder — very refreshing.

• *Slather on calamine lotion.* Be gentle but generous with it and your burn will soon burn less.

• *Avoid hot and cold conditions.* That means no hot showers or baths, which will only increase your pain. And because a sunburn causes a loss of body heat, don't go into air-conditioned rooms or you'll get a bad case of the chills.

• *Take two aspirin and take to bed.* You'll feel better in the morning.

EIGHT

Makeup Magic

Put on makeup like a pro and let a prettier you shine through. With just the right touch of makeup, which means a *light* touch of makeup, you can look and feel better about yourself. One small change — maybe a new shade of lipstick, eye shadow smoothed on in a new way, or blusher brushed on with a new stroke — can do it.

Always aim for a natural look and you can't go wrong. When it comes to makeup, it's possible to have too much of a good thing. What ought to stand out when you're through applying your makeup, are your best features rather than the colors on your face. So learn to play up your eye color, your long lashes, your lips, your nose, or whatever you consider worth calling attention to. Makeup can make your good points even better.

What about your less than ideal features? What if you think your eyes are too small, your brows too pale, your lips too thin, or your nose too wide? There are a few tricks you can try to correct or minimize small flaws, but you can't really change any feature in a big way with makeup alone. So why waste time worrying about the negative? Instead, emphasize the positive — your assets — and make the most of them. Remember, nobody's perfect, not even the most sought-after models. They work with what they've got, and so should you. Coming up, all the ways to do it with makeup.

How to give yourself a makeover

Before you can learn to apply makeup, you must first know how to select makeup. Every item should suit your skin's needs and flatter your complexion. Of course, you have to have the right tools, and use them correctly. Step by step, here's how to make yourself over, with details on choosing and using the basics you need.

Step one: face cleansing

It wouldn't make sense to paint a pretty watercolor on a dirty canvas. It also doesn't make sense to put makeup on a face that isn't freshly washed and super-clean. Simply follow the cleansing routine for your skin type.

Step two: moisturizing

Oily or dry, whatever your skin type, moisturizer is a must. The oilier your skin, the lighter your moisturizer should be. It doesn't actually penetrate your skin, since no moisturizer can do that. But it does protect it. That's because moisturizer seals in your skin's own natural moisture, preventing it from evaporating. A moisturizer also acts as a barrier against the grime and pollutants in the air, which can clog up your pores, causing blackheads or pimples.

Choose a moisturizer for your skin type. Even if your skin is very oily, a very light moisturizer is essential to give you a fresh, healthy glow and protect your skin.

How to apply: Spread a light film of moisturizer, evenly, all over your face and neck using your fingertips. Smooth on as little moisturizer as possible. Then, if your skin is on the oily side, blot with a tissue.

Step three: putting on a base

Makeup base, or foundation, should be used only if your skin tone is very uneven, blotchy, or not all one color. Use it sparingly. Too much may lead to breakouts, especially if your skin is oily.

When you go to a store to buy foundation, don't wear any makeup at all. Select the shades that look as if they are close to your natural skin color and test each one on your face and neck, never on your hands or wrists where your skin may be very different. You're looking for an almost perfect match.

Don't ever try to drastically change your skin color using foundation. It can't be done. Pale faces will not look tan, olive complexions will not look rosy, for example, with foundation — merely overly made up. So go with your skin color. Every shade of skin can be beautiful, so don't fight it.

How to apply: Using your fingertips, gently spread a very thin coat of foundation only on those areas of your face that really need some cover-up. Be sure to blend it carefully, especially around the neck area (check your side view). You probably don't need a foundation all over your face, and definitely not around your eyes.

Never rub on a foundation, or use a sponge. Even if you wash a sponge after you use it, you can't get it spotlessly clean. A sponge also spreads grease, grime, and bacteria from one part of your face to another, particularly awful if your skin is acne-prone.

Step four: stroking on blush

Smile. That's the apple of your cheek, where the flesh goes up. Blush belongs on your cheekbones, not below. Put it on in the wrong spot, and you won't get its full benefit, which is to give you a natural-looking flush of color.

Incorrect placement is a common mistake, as is choosing an incorrect color. What's your most flattering color? The color of your cheeks when you blush, or when you've just come in from the cold and have a healthy glow. Always choose the softest, most subtle color, nothing dramatic. Then, when you want a deeper color on your cheeks for those times when your skin is tan, or when you're going someplace very special, you can simply put on a little extra.

How to apply: Stroke it on with a brush, which should, of course, be washed regularly. Blend well. Or, if your skin is oily, use a cotton ball and throw it away. And here's a trick for tanned faces: Your color will look even better if you not only put blush on your cheeks, but also a touch on your forehead, chin, and the bridge of your nose, the spots where the sun hits your face.

Step five: coloring your eyes

To accent or complement the color of your eyes, a touch of shadow is next. For everyday, a light brown or a subtle blue will do the trick. Actually, brown or blue eyes can carry off almost any shade successfully, from pale pink and lavender to the deepest earthy brown. But if you have one of those in-between eye colors, you'll just have to experiment until you find the most flattering shadow color for you. Keep in mind that you don't have to match your eye color. In fact, sometimes a contrasting color accentuates your eyes more. So if you have green eyes, don't necessarily go for green shadow, and if you have blue eyes, try something different.

When choosing eye makeup, or any kind of makeup, there's one basic rule to remember: Colors that are light or shiny always bring areas forward and so make a feature more noticeable. Colors that are dark or smoky, with no shine (called matte), make an area appear to recede, so a feature is less noticeable. Once you understand that, you know how to choose and use eye colors to flatter the shape of your eyes.

How to apply:

• *Small eyes* will seem larger with a light or shiny shadow on the lids. On the brow bone, just above the lids, smudge on a slightly darker shade — maybe a light grey or warm brown — starting in the center and extending out beyond your lids just a bit. Never use eye liner.

• *Deep-set eyes* also appear to come forward with a bright, light, or shiny shadow on the lids. On the brow bone, just above the lids, put a slightly darker shade from corner to corner. Never use eyeliner but do use mascara — preferably black. One more tip: Keep your eyebrows on the thin side, but not extremely thin, so that they don't overpower your eyes. Pluck often so they look neat.

• *Prominent eyes* will seem to recede with a dark, matte shadow on the lids and on the brow bone, just above and close to the lids. Don't use eyeliner, and use mascara only sparingly. Tip: Your eyebrows should be neither too thin nor too thick, nothing exaggerated. If they're sparse or fair, fill in with a pencil in a color that matches your own.

• *Close-set eyes* will look farther apart with light shadow on the outer half of the lids and on the outer half of the brow bone, just above the lids. Tip: Pluck your brows so that they don't point down toward your nose. They should run straight across. Also pluck them in the center so that they are a little beyond the inner corner of your eyes. Do keep them neat, and on the thin side — but not too thin.

• *Wide-apart* eyes appear to be closer together with a dark, matte shadow on the inner half of the lids and the inner half of the brow bone, close to the nose. Tip: If possible, allow your brows to grow so that they extend out a bit beyond the inside corner of your eyes.

And here are some final words of advice: Before you apply eye makeup, be sure your eye area is clean and dry, and your shadow will go on smoothly, evenly. If there's a trace of moisturizer or cleansing cream on your eyes, your makeup will quickly smear and run. Also, always blend your shadow well, using your fingertips or the applicator or a cotton swab. Sharp, definite edges look unnatural and unattractive.

Step six: brushing on mascara

Just a little mascara can really bring out your eyes, make them sparkle and look wider. You may find, for everyday, all you need on your eyes is one thin coat of mascara — nothing else at all. It's important, however, to choose and use mascara correctly. You don't want a harsh look, or cakey, clumpy lashes, or dark smudges and black flecks around your eyes.

Always choose black or brown mascara, never an unnatural color. Brown is usually best for those who have light-colored hair; black is for those with dark hair or very dark brows and lashes. But even if your hair is light, you may like the way black mascara accents your lashes — it's up to you.

How to apply: Start by curling your lashes with an eyelash curler. Your mascara will cling better and your lashes appear a bit thicker, if you then put a very light dusting of loose powder on your lashes. Another trick to make your lashes seem thicker: First apply your mascara to the top of your lashes, brushing down, then from underneath, brushing up. Always use the brush slowly and carefully, covering each lash evenly.

When the mascara is thoroughly dry, use a small eyelash brush to separate each hair and get out any unsightly clumps, so your lashes will look fuller. Use a second coat only for special occasions. And if you do, be sure the first coat is dry.

If you find that black mascara is too dark but brown too light, mix them. Simply brush on the brown mascara then use the black only for the tips.

Or, if you don't like the look of mascara, just brush your lashes with a little petroleum jelly — they'll really shine, and appear darker, too.

Step seven: coloring your lips

Match your lipstick to your blush, and the result will be a soft, pretty look. For luscious-looking lips and a richer, more vibrant color, finish off with lip gloss. Some are tinted — you may not want to wear lipstick with them at all.

How to apply: If you like to wear lip colors that are either dark or very bright, always use a lip brush. Just outline your lips and fill in with the same color.

If your lips are thin, first outline your lips, following their natural shape, with a slightly darker shade of lip color or pencil. Second, fill in with the lighter lipstick. Finally, blend very well so that the line is almost invisible.

Gloss makes thin lips look fuller, too. And here's a tip: The brighter and lighter your lip color, the fuller your lips will appear. So to make full lips seem thinner, go for a dark shade.

Step eight: finishing touches

If your skin is dry, powder may be all wrong for you. You can get a glowing, dewy look with this trick: Soak a cotton ball in cool water, squeeze out excess moisture, then dab the cotton ball all over your face. Or you can fill a spray bottle with mineral water and spritz your face very lightly.

Now for the big finish, the final test: Stand back and look at your face in a mirror. If all you see is makeup, if anything you've used on your face looks harsh and unnatural, then you've made a mistake somewhere. Simply start all over again until you find the makeup that's right for you.

Tips and tricks

Turn up the Light. When you're putting on makeup, it's essential that you see exactly what you're doing. That means the lighting near your mirror must be good. Natural lighting is best since there's less distortion of color, and most of the time the world will be viewing you in sunlight. But if you can't possibly put your makeup mirror near a window, after you apply your makeup carry a small hand mirror to a window and check yourself out. Does your makeup look natural in natural light? If so, you've done a first-rate job.

Oil Tamer. It's a good idea, if your skin is oily and blotchy, to use only enough foundation to even out your skin tone. Then blot your makeup using a clean tissue. Finally, a light dusting of transparent, loose powder on your T-zone to set your makeup and fight shine.

Blush for Black Skin. The darker your skin tone, the deeper the shade of blush you should use. If you have light toned skin, stay away from blushes with yellow tones, which will make you look sallow.

Nose Shapers. You can make your nose appear slightly thinner, or fuller, with a little corrective makeup. For a large, wide nose use a somewhat darker foundation on the sides, above the nostrils — and do blend well. For a thin nose, a light foundation on the sides will make it seem fuller. Of course, blend very well so no sharp line of makeup shows.

Tweezing. Don't overdo. The no-eyebrow look is attractive on very few people. Try to follow your natural brow shape. As a rule, brows should be almost the same width all the way across, tapering only slightly at the outer edges. Where should the eyebrow begin and end? Hold a pencil straight up from your nostril — that's where it ought to begin. Then hold the pencil from your nostril to the other corner of your eyelid to your eyebrow — that's where it ought to end.

How to tweeze: Pluck in the direction of hair growth, always one hair at a time. While you tweeze, use a small toothbrush or eyebrow brush and constantly brush your eyebrows up and down, shaping them as you go. This shows you their natural shape so you can see what should and should not be plucked. Never tweeze the hairs above your brows. And after you tweeze, soothe your skin by dabbing on rubbing alcohol or witch hazel with a cotton ball.

Tip for unruly brows: Don't overpluck. Instead, keep them down by brushing them with a little petroleum jelly, or spritz hair spray on your eyebrow brush and shape, or run a wet finger over soap and smooth down the hairs.

If you use eyebrow pencil to fill in any sparse spots, be sure the shade you choose matches your brows exactly. And when applying, use light, feathery strokes so the result will look very natural.

Makeup can be magic. But only if you use it the right way — to make beautiful skin even more beautiful.